Y0-CKL-264

If Only In A Dream
Short Stories and Poems

J Lee Brown

Bloomington, IN  Milton Keynes, UK

AuthorHouse™
1663 Liberty Drive, Suite 200
Bloomington, IN 47403
www.authorhouse.com
Phone: 1-800-839-8640

AuthorHouse™ UK Ltd.
500 Avebury Boulevard
Central Milton Keynes, MK9 2BE
www.authorhouse.co.uk
Phone: 08001974150

© 2006 J Lee Brown. All rights reserved.

No part of this book may be reproduced, stored in a retrieval system, or transmitted by any means without the written permission of the author.

First published by AuthorHouse 9/21/2006

ISBN: 1-4259-2270-8 (e)
ISBN: 1-4259-2269-4 (sc)

Library of Congress Control Number: 2006902844

Printed in the United States of America
Bloomington, Indiana

This book is printed on acid-free paper.

This book is dedicated to my children,
Tracy, Tiffany and Rachel
Who have never left me

And to my parents
Johnny and Sooky Crist
Who never left willingly.

My love and admiration to all of them
who are and were -
far more talented than I.

Table of Contents

Littlest Angel	1
My Mama was a Bellamy	3
A Tribute To An Elder	16
The Pantry	19
The Horn Player	39
The Pirate Story	43
If Only In A Dream	55
Teach Them To Fish……	57
Freedom Cage	75

Littlest Angel

I can hear her voice outside now
"there was nothing we could do"
Why is Mommy crying?
What did that doctor do?
I wonder if she's angry
Cause there's so many people here
Mosquitoes on the screen door
"be still the baby's near"
they're looking at me sadly
"she'll never understand"
where did you go this morning?
"Come baby, take my hand"
you know when I kissed Daddy
he said he'd be right home
he was going to the doctor
then we'd get an ice cream cone
It's okay don't cry Mom
I'm not hungry anyway
All these people sittin' here
Been bringin' food all day.
I guess you're going to tell me
what I'm way too young to hear
That's what they've all been saying
But I know you'll make it clear
There won't be any pony rides?
You mean I'll have to ride alone?
But if I really was his angel
Why'd he leave me at home???

My Mama was a Bellamy

My Mama was a Bellamy. Never really knew what that meant even though I heard it all my life. But now as I stand in this yard, behind this grand ol' house, it's beginning to hit me, what being a Bellamy must have meant to my mother. I hear the tour guide talking. Telling of the dimensions of the kitchen, and how by the pulling of a cord, the servants would hear a bell ring in other parts of the house. I stand here, anonymously, knowing I could interrupt at any point, and change everyone's day. But it is becoming a humorous game, how many things she is getting right and wrong. I spent my summers here before this child was born. I could correct her at any moment, but she is actually doing such a great job, bringing such an illusion of grandeur to this place, I can't even speak. That we were all somehow so proper and such an elite part of society, my Gran would be proud. I am rather taken back however. It is so warm today and I really need to sit down. I didn't think coming here would affect me so. I look behind me at the stairs going up from the yard to the porch and feel driven to walk up them. I ease away from the group unnoticed, and walk up the stairs like a 7-year-old child. Without hesitation I know to go to the left, to the curved stairway hidden behind a door. Oh yes, I can sit here. There is a cool breeze flowing down the stairs. Me and Moezella's daughter Tess, Nathaniel and Sam (they were Mary Ann's boys) played on these stairs everyday. Moezella, Mary Ann, and Joanie took care of the children. Joanie was young herself. She would even help with plays and talent shows that we put on. I didn't know then that they were slaves, or that Tess, Nathaniel, and Sam were too. I didn't even know what that meant. I don't think the children did either. We were just children having fun. None of us even had chores to do, except to stay out of everybody's way. The curved stairway went from the second floor (where the grown up bedrooms were) all the way to the basement (where the kitchen and dining room were). We played on that beautiful curved stairway all the time! We'd make believe we were Kings and Queens walking down the stairs holding on to that curved railing. Why, I remember one time Ms. Sarah, chasing us out of there with a broom, and grabbing Nathaniel and taking him to his Mama Mary Ann. Nathaniel had decided me and Tess needed robes to be Queen, so he took two sheets off Ms. Sarah's clothes line and we had tied them around our necks, dragging them up and down those wooden stairs. She was coming up from the kitchen to take Ms. Ellen some tea, and not looking down, had stepped on the bottom of the sheet that was tied around Tess' neck. I saw Tess kind of gag, and then she started falling backwards and fell right into Ms. Sarah. The tea went all over Ms. Sarah's starched white apron, and me and Tess and Sam ran up those stairs so fast, all the way to the Belvedere and hid up there until supper time. Tess said wasn't nothing to be scared about. She was always so brave. We'd pull boxes up to the windows in the Belvedere, and look out all over the city. She would talk about the day she was gonna leave North Carolina. She was gonna be a writer in New York City she'd say. Knowing Tess – I bet she probably did it.

I hear the voice of another tour guide. She is taking another group to the yard. I hear her talking about the "slave quarters". I get a slight pain in my heart listening to this, because my memories serve me well. Me and Tess, and Nathaniel and Sam played in that yard, I guess in our own little world. Sometimes Ms. Sarah would bring clothes out in the yard on hot days, to wash them. She'd make us all Sassafras tea and sugar cookies, and would sit out there and sing the prettiest songs. She had a beautiful voice. Mr. Guy (who drove the coaches, and Big Tony who was always fixing things) would sometimes come out and sing with her. We would gather the berries we had gotten from the vines on the side of the house, and sit in the very doors of those "slave quarters" and just watch the show. My mama often came outside too, even in the prettiest of her dresses, and would pull a wooden box over and help Ms. Sarah wash those clothes. She even tried to sing along once, but Ms. Sarah started laughing so hard, as did Mr. Guy and Big Tony, it made my Mama start laughing too. Don't get me wrong now. My mother had a beautiful voice, but one for the Opera, not for "Down By the Riverside" I am telling you that noise that came out of my mama's mouth that day scared little Sam so bad he ran under the house and hid in the crawl space. No one could stop laughing. I remember Ms Sarah finally jumpin' up and runnin' for the privie, talkin' about she couldn't "hold herself". Mama looked up the big stairs behind her, still laughing and crying, she grabbed the bottom of her dress and ran after Ms. Sarah and ran in the privie right after her. She was just laughing and running talking about how she couldn't hold herself either. I can still hear the two of them laughin' from the privie.

'Of course it wasn't always that way. Sometimes the real world crept into our back yard and would try to spoil everything. Like the night my Daddy came from Alabama to visit. Him and my Grandfather didn't get along. That is why me and Mama would come alone for the summer. Grandfather would allow him to come for a visit, but he never stayed long. It had been a long day of playing and me and Tess had already had our baths, but it was so warm up on the children's floor, Mama said me and Tess could go out in the yard. We decided to go up to what I knew as "Tess' house". Ms. Sarah was still working in the kitchen in the big house, and Moezella and Mary Ann were still tending to the other children up on the children's floor. Me and Tess and Joanie were telling stories and had fallen asleep. That brick building was under the trees and was always cooler than Gran's house. My Daddy had arrived with quite an entrance I guess, demanding to see me. When my mother said I was out in the back with Tess and Joanie in the "Servant's

Quarters", he went flying out the back door screaming and yellin' at my mother about the indecency of it all that she was allowing me to wallow in the dirt with the slaves. My grandmother heard the ruckus and ran down the servant stairs (as she often did, but you won't hear the tour guide tell that!) and ran right into my father! He stepped into a pale behind him and fell right down all those back stairs banging his head on the side of the well. By this time Tess, and Joanie and me woke up and my father was lying at the bottom of the stairs and his head was kind of cocked up against the stones of the well. The doctor came, my Daddy had broken his foot. Me and Tess heard the Doctor say if he had had less of the spirits in him he wouldn't have fallen. Me and Tess decided that must mean my Daddy was so full of the Holy Spirit Ms. Sarah always talked about that he jumped off the porch. What ever it was, I'll never forget Gran's face as she stood at the top of those stairs looking down at my Daddy after he fell. When he was coming to, she got a true look of disappointment on her face. Tess said Gran was wishing he was dead. When my Daddy sat up she yelled down to him in her dignified way, and told him God punished him for insulting her family. That these "servants", as he called them, were more family than him, and to kindly leave her home. Daddy was gone the next morning. It wasn't until later in the summer that I realized it wasn't the "Holy" spirit that was in my Daddy that night. The whole spirit subject came up again when Nathaniel and Sam snuck some of Mr. Guy's "spirits" out of the coach house one night and were drinking it like crazy until poor little Sam got sick. Moezella found them in the privie. Sam got put to bed with a pot next to his bed, and Nathaniel got another whippin', and Tess and me made a pact we would never touch this spirit stuff. I never broke our pact to this day. I bet Tess never has either.

There were other times that the real world tried to crash into ours. Like the day we talked Mama into letting us (me, Tess, Nathaniel, and Sam) walk down to the corner store to get some penny candy. I remember my Aunt telling Mama it wasn't a good idea. I just figured she didn't want us to have fun, ever. Mama won the argument and off we went. We were just having a time walking to the store with our 5 pennies each that Gran had given us. We got to the door of the store, and opened it, and there was a lady with a big hat and a fancy dress and she leaned over and whispered something to Mr. Evans. He walked out from around the counter up to the door. He tells me I can come in but Tess and the boys have to wait outside till the lady in the big hat leaves. Right then, Mr. John E. Taylor walked up (he owned the shoe store) and I stopped him. I said, "Mr. Taylor, Sir, you can't go in there right now." He said, "Why not, child?" I said, "Cause there is a big lady in there, with a big dress, and a big hat, and I guess there ain't enough room." He looked up at Mr. Evans and said, "Is that right Mr. Evans? Is the lady's hat too big for the children to fit in your store?" Mr. Evans said I must not of heard him right and let us all in to buy our candy. The big hatted lady stormed out of the store. Funny thing was when she stormed out her big hat caught on the bell by the door, and grabbed hold of the big ol' hat and nearly ripped her head off. We couldn't help but laugh. (even Mr. Taylor laughed). We scooted out of there right quick so we wouldn't get blamed for nothing. I remember thinking the whole thing strange. The way Mr. Evans said I didn't hear him right. Tess said I did hear him right. She said Mr. John E. Taylor worked for the Mayor of Wilmington, and the Mayor didn't like ladies with big hats, and that's why Mr. Evans changed his story! We laughed and ate our candy and walked on home. But once we told Mama the story , I heard my Auntie say "I told you so" to my Mama and Gran hit her fist down on the kitchen table and walked out of the room. That was the end of our adventures out side our yard.

I am gettin' achy in my bones sittin' here on these steps. I want to go up to the children's floor one time quick to look at the stage. I hear the tour group now walking down the proper stairs to the first floor, so I'll sneak up the servant's stairs to the second floor, and quietly tip toe up the only flight of stairs to the children's floor. And there it is! The stage.

I grab a chair from Joanie's room (she slept up here with the children). As I sit here, in this big wide hallway, I can almost hear the giggles and laughter. We had a big tub to take baths in down by Joanie's room, and I remember one of the babies getting away from Joanie and running out here in the hallway soaking wet. Joanie ran after him and slipped in the water he had left on the floor, and slid on her petticoats smack dab into the bottom of the stage. Backside first. It makes me laugh even now. And these windows! Out here in the middle of the hall. They opened up from the bedrooms on to the hallway. It was funny to us, but Gran always said that the windows were to make the breezes blow between the bedrooms before they flowed up to the Belvedere. It was just one more thing for us to do. We crawled through them to go from room to room, instead of using the doors. That is obviously why they were there, or so it seemed to us.

The stage was an architectural error. (Something else they don't know!) My Mama heard the argument between Mr. James Post (the architect) and my grandfather. It had to do with the way they built the roof, and it left this big platform about three feet off the floor at the end of this big wide hallway. They were going to seal it up, but Gran (quite the Thespian) decided it would be a great place for the children to play, and play we did! We had all kinds of plays and talent shows. One time we actually got the neighborhood kids to come and we charged admission. We even got my Grandfather to pay! We got that idea from Mama. She told us stories about the plays her and her brothers and sisters use to put on right there on that same stage! They made Grandfather pay too!

I think my fondest memory was the night we had finished one of our great productions, and we begged Sarah to sing. All of us kids jumped down from the stage and sat on the floor in front of the grown-ups. Grandfather was sitting to my right. Sarah walked up and sat on the stage. (Grown ups couldn't stand up on it, that was what made it so special!) Mr. Guy had his mandolin, and sat at her feet. She began singing and Mr. Guy started playing. I remember watching Ms. Sarah's face, and seeing a tear run down her cheek as she sang, and then my Grandfather started wiping his eyes with a handkerchief. Me and Tess just knew that those beautiful sounds were just floating right up the stairs to the Belvedere and through the windows and out into the city. Probably everyone in Wilmington was crying that night, right along with my Grandfather and Ms. Sarah. It seemed that they were crying about much more than that pretty song, but then that's probably another story.

"Excuse me ma'am! What are you doing up here! You are much too old to have been climbing all those stairs alone! The tours are over and we are closing up. You have to go! I am sure you don't want to stay in this empty old house!"

Hmmm. As I get up, I have to laugh.

"This house may be old like me, but it will never be empty. There are so many stories to tell, there will be someone in every room as long as I can remember – My Mama was a Bellamy!"

A Tribute To An Elder

You walk past me in the morning – oh so swiftly
I speak to you – oh so softly...
You're on such a busy schedule – but you stop
      And smile...and speak back to me...
You must know...
      That I once walked swiftly in the morning, too
I sit sometimes and wonder – if anyone knows
I had a busy schedule only a few years ago, myself.

I'm in this chair with wheels and can't quite get thru the door..
I struggle and I push 'til tears come to my eyes –
      I use to run to catch a trolley – and push my way thru any crowd
      The tears come – uninvited – as I give up..
And then I feel your arms hugging me –
You must know I never gave up – only a few years ago.

You look at me and try to encourage the smile and enthusiasm you have....
You want me to laugh and have another good time for you –
You try so hard during your 8 to 10 hour day
To make my life better for me
Listen child – I have had a beautiful life!

I have learned many lessons – and still learn more each day –
I have loved with all my heart – and still have love to

give away
I have laughed until I am silly – and I have cried the whole night long
I have screamed from mountain tops – I have sung your song
I have reached some of my goals-and still have some to go
I have traveled many miles, and oh! I loved it so!
I have given many speeches for a thousand ears to hear-
And have thrown a football and heard the mighty cheer
I have held my daughter in the palm of my hand-
And I have heard the war cry on foreign lands
I have walked the isle to say my wedding vows-
And I have stood upon the stage and taken my big bow

So listen, closely children – as you look at me today-
While you see me sitting here – with hair that's thin and gray
Look beyond my wrinkles, and my shaking hand-
Look beyond my whispers and the plastic hospital band,
And see me as the person – like the one you are today –
    The one that cries, and loves, and laughs....

    The one that swiftly walks away.

The Pantry

The way the story was always told to me was that my grandmother was stolen by the gypsies when she was a young girl and how brave my great grandfather was because he chased them down (those thieves and scoundrels!), and single handidly retrieved his baby daughter and brought her back home to her distraught mother, and Oh, how the family rejoiced! OH PLEASE! The woman was hateful! If the gypsies were truly thieves and scoundrels they would have deserved her! My sisters and I would joke through the years about that very concept! She had always been very mean to us, and repeatedly through our lives voiced her disdain of how useless we all were. My useless sister, who had her fine arts degree, and attended all the Inaugural Balls in D.C. with her wealthy husband. My other worthless sister was a registered nurse and became a flight nurse being flown into Critical Care Units around the country. Then me, okay, two out of three ain't bad! But back to the story!

My grandparents had long passed away, and my mother was going to rent out their house and my sister and I were left to clean it out. We had made our way to the basement that day and there were two little rooms there in the back of the basement with big wooden doors. One was an old coal room, and still had the coal shoot coming down from the window. For you young ones, that was the way we use to heat our houses. Coal was brought to the house in a big truck and then the coal man would pour coal down the shoot, then it was up to the man of the house to keep coal in the furnace. The other little room was a pantry. My sister took the main part of the basement and started going through the boxes, and she assigned me to the little pantry room. Interesting as it was, and as many times as I had snuck in there as a child to hide from my sisters, today it was spooky! I took boxes in there and flipped on the one hanging light bulb, and started taking things off the shelves. Old vases, a toaster, jars of apple butter, my goodness! That apple butter must have been fifty years old! (If Granny 'd been alive, she probably would have tried to feed it to us!) I gradually worked my way down to the corner of the shelves and moved a big ugly statue of a Japanese man. I remembered being so scared of that thing as a child. It use to sit in the extra bedroom on a book case facing the bed. So when we had to stay all night at my grandma's house, you went to sleep with him staring at you. When I got old enough, I would put him in the closet, and put him back on the shelf in the morning before my grandmother came in the room. So, now as I stared at this monster man for a moment, and picked him up, to place him in the goodwill box, a tightly rapped package fell out of the bottom of him! It was about the size of a small book, wrapped in purple suede material bound with thin brown leather straps. It fell right into my hands. It scared me so badly I threw it to the floor, and of course I threw the Japanese man right along with it! I am afraid he met his demise that day on the concrete floor of the pantry! My heart was beating so fast, I remember thinking finally this old Japanese man is going to get his revenge for all his nights in the closet. I am going to die of a heart failure in this pantry, in this basement, of this old empty house, and no one will know he killed me! Then my sister opened the door and ask me what I was doing! Why was I screaming?

"I was screaming? I said to her. "I guess I couldn't hear myself over the POUNDING OF MY HEART!!!!"

I tried to stop screeching at her and explain what happened while she accused me of breaking the old Japanese man on purpose.

"You always hated him! You expect me to believe....", and then she stopped talking and bent down. "What is this?", she said like I would know!

She reached over me and picked up the purple suede package. I told her I didn't know and that it had fallen out of the Japanese man. She sat down on a box, and started to open it. This is how we always get in trouble I thought to myself. If she wasn't sticking her toe, her head, or her fingers in something, she was always opening up stuff we weren't suppose to! So she begins unwrapping the thin brown straps, and unfolds the purple suede cloth, and finds the object wrapped once more in a red scarf, with little gold ropes around it. Now I was really getting scared! What had we found? She untied the little gold ropes, and removed the scarf. There was a little book and a box. The little book was some type of journal. When my sister opened the box, it was a deck of Tarot cards. Very old, yellowed tarot cards. Did I mention my grandmother's name was on the box? Well, at least kind of. It said

"TO Marianna Louisa, with love, Mama".

Louisa? Who was Louisa? My grandmother's name was Marian Beaufant There was no middle name, and it was Marian, not Marianna! She had no middle name! She told me that herself! She said her mother didn't believe in middle names. "They are frivolous indulgences to make one sound more important than they are". Well, okay Louisa! As my sister began to look at the little book, she looked terror-stricken and she kind of slid against the wall.

She said, "Oh, dear sister, you better sit down! You aren't going to believe this!"

I remember asking if it was Grandma's journal.

She said, "No, it is written "to her" by her mother". I said, "Grandma Beaufant? Grandma's mother?"

She said, "Well you are half right. Her mother yes, but her name was not Grandma Beaufant, it was Louisa Romanov, according to this".

Now I was the one sliding to the floor, and this is what she read:

"Things you should know, from your mother with love. Louisa Fredrika Gustav Romanov. My dear Daughter, I have kept many things from you, for your protection. I know today you are 14 years old, a woman about to begin your life. I have waited until this day to disclose information to you, for your further guidance and protection. Your father vowed to me, he would give this to you on your 14th birthday, so if you are reading this, he kept his promise. I should start from the beginning. You are not of French decent, and you are not a Beaufant. Your birth name is Marianna Louisa Romanov. Your father and I were both born in Romania, of the Ludar, we are of the Rom.

"ROM! "I said, "the Rom are gypsies!"

"How do you know that", my sister says.

"German History, we studied about the Third Reich in college. The Rom, or Gypsies, were among the many people persecuted during World War II. Go on keep reading!"

She continues:

"Your father's name was Serge' Romanov, and he stowed us away on a ship he had been working on as a laborer. Our lifestyle of traveling and happiness had come to and end in Romania. We had begun a life of running and hiding. There had been a major coup' in Romania, and the Czar had proclaimed war on the Rom, because we did not own land. We lived a traveling life, and we did not pay taxes. Your father, Serge' would say, "Why should I pay taxes? Most of the roads were built by our people, either voluntarily, or as imprisoned slaves. We have paid more than our share!" Well as one would guess, this Romanian population of Gypsies (as outsiders say) was a very large family. A large population that is not sharing it's wealth with the Czar! So we become as a people, the focus of his attention. We were hunted as dogs, and if they caught us they would take the whole family and display us with in the city gates, tied to poles, and let the townspeople do as they will. I won't describe the humiliation and desecration those brothers and sisters of ours faced as you are a young lady, and need good thoughts in your mind only. When the "Hunting of Gypsies" took on a reward from the Czar, things became perilous and I was with child. I could not keep up with the constant running. In normal times, if someone with in the Rom was with child the entire tribe entered into what we called "nesting". We would find a good field, outside the city limits, that had a water supply, and we would set up camp there, until the child was born. The Baro (the head of the family) would always negotiate the stay with the landowner, so we would live in peace. The men would help the landowner with his crops, or his herds, to pay for our time there. This is an important point for you to understand. We were not thieves. We paid our way! At least in Romania. The "Tricks of Gypsies" began in the Americas, and they only began because of the life we were forced to live. We were not allowed to own land, or work, or grow crops. So we were forced to use our main commodity, our clever minds. Some seemed to be more clever than others, but always more clever than the Outsiders, who always seemed to be running things. With a new child coming, things had gotten so bad for the tribe, nesting would have put them all in danger, so your father decided we should go to the Americas. His cousin and brother were already there. He wrote them of our condition, and his brother said nesting was still a custom being done there, and the tribe was willing to take on that responsibility if we came to them. We had no choice. So, your father paid many rubles to a Russian seaman and he slipped us into the cargo bay of a big ship leaving in the morning. I must tell you daughter, it was a grueling trip. The area we were confined to was the size of a small closet. It had water seeping in on the floor and no heat of course. We couldn't speak all day long so our presence would not be revealed. To make matters worse I was getting sick from the motion of the ship. Your father worried greatly for the welfare of you and I, and many days Serge would not eat so I could sustain your life. Even though you were not born yet, your father always said he must feed his little princess. He knew you would be a girl! When we pulled in to the port in America, your Uncle Romi was waiting for us right there on the dock. He waited until deep into the night, because we had to sneak off the ship. When we finally got to him, he took us by a buckboard and horse to the camp. There everyone was waiting for us, with so much food and music, it was like a dream come true. We had just settled down and began sharing stories of the old country, and this my child is where the dream comes to an end. As we were resting and talking, a large group of men rode up on horseback. The Bora and the other men in the camp jumped up and stood in front of the women, and asked what they wanted. One of the men on the horses jumped down yelling "there he is, there he is, there is the stow away!" He pointed at your father and they all drew their guns. Two men rode their horses very fast up beside where your father was standing, and grabbed him and wisked him away into the forest. It was the last time I saw your father. As they disappeared into the forest, we heard gunfire, and we heard the horses ride away. When we ran to where we heard the shots, there was nothing there. We never even found his body. That was my welcome to America. I had three months of nesting to go, so the tribe pulled farther into the wilderness (a day or so away) and we camped there until you were born. A month later we broke camp and moved farther west. It was then I was taught the "tricks of the gypsies" and the ways of "making the coins". We found that people would pay for the many things we did for fun. The Ludar were show people and we loved to entertain, sing and dance. So we would sing, and dance for the outsiders and make many coins for it. Outsiders would also pay for the Knowledge in the cards. (Isn't that funny? They would pay us to play a simple game we played as children?) They believed all the long-winded stories we told, and they paid us to tell them. Even in the old country we were known as storytellers! Why would anyone ever believe us? We were just having fun! But I guess there lies the trick! We went on traveling with the tribe, you and I, for about two more years until Uncle Romi's wife was with child, and we were in a territory of many lakes. We had been nesting for a few months and the man that allowed us to camp on his land was an exceptionally kind man. He was a very tall, elegant looking man, that owned a barbershop and a boarding house in the town there. He grew wheat and corn on his land and always provided our people with plenty. We within the Rom would call him a "Romany Rye". It meant he spent time with the Rom people and spoke our language. It was a good peaceful time. He had many children of his own and he allowed them to play with our children, and often invited our children to his house. We would joke many times about how we could take all of his children with us, as they were all dark, and looked like children of the Rom. He would joke back and say to please take them. He was the nicest outsider I had ever met. He was fascinated with our abilities, and respected our way of life. I had begun to not feel well, my legs were giving me a great deal of pain, and I was slowly finding it hard to walk. The pain would sometimes go all the way to my head, and I could not move from my cot. When I was called to work, (my days to share in the support of the tribe) I was found lacking, and was becoming burdensome to the rest of the tribe. Others were having to care for you during the day and our portions were becoming gifts rather than wages earned. As a true Ludar of the Rom, your love is for your people. The harvest was over, and Uncle Romi's child had been born, the nesting day had ended. (At least for them.) I knew I could not continue on with them, because I would slow them down, and possibly endanger the entire tribe. I wrote a note to the man who owned the land we were camping on, (the Romany Rye), asking him only if I could sell him some of the jewels I had from the old country that I had actually saved to hand down to you. I had not asked him for anything else. I sent the note to him through his older child who had been visiting me quite regularly. I had even taught her some of our games. Well, that very evening the man came with his carriage to the camp, and spoke with your Uncle Romi, and then they came to me. By this time, it was common knowledge that I would not live to see your womanhood. This man offered to take you and I to his home, where his wife and daughters would care for us, and he would raise you with his own. And each year, when the tribe came through for the Harvest work, they would always be able to visit with you, and you would learn our way. Although I had never lived among any other kind of people, and it would be a harsh adjustment (I had heard that Outsiders don't put any spice in their foods) it seemed to be the only solution to our most perilous condition. After my demise, at least you would not be an orphan earner in the tribe. Without parents, the orphan earners can fall into a very troubled life. With no inheritance, you become last in line for most things, and can be overpowered to share your earnings, or lose them completely, and forced to live a rationed life. A life your father would have hated for his Princess Child. So, I accepted the Romany Rye's offer. That evening we rode on the buckboard to his house, and we were taken into the house and given a whole room of our own. The man and his wife had learned a lot from our people. Knowing how much the night's stars meant to us, he gave us a room that opened up onto a garden.

He had a chair in the room waiting for me that he had attached wheels to. Each night his daughter would wheel me outside to the garden that overlooked the very field we had camped in with the family, rap you up in a summer blanket and lay you in my lap and leave us there to fall asleep. Then sometime in the night, they would come back, and put us in the big down bed, and we woke up together. The patio doors would be open, and the birds would be chirping, and the sun would be shining in on us. They were such a kind and loving family. I lived through one more harvest. What a grand time we had! The Ludar came through, your Uncle Romi and everyone. What a delight to see the whole family! They stayed with us for two whole months! They didn't camp at the edge of the field, this time they camped right outside our bedroom door! You ran freely between our room and the camp, as did all the children. I think the Romany Rye and his family spent more time in the camp than they did in the house. They would eat their meals with the tribe, and sit around the fire. Your Uncle Romi taught the Rye man to play the mandolin, and they would play old Romanian songs together, while everyone sang. Those were joyous days, even though they were sad ones, because we all knew my time was short. But my heart was full of love for my people, and I was at peace knowing you would be safe. You would still learn about your ancestors and your people, so there was great joy in my heart. I knew bringing you to the Americas was the right decision. I never agreed with the tricks of the gypsies, at least the ones that caused harm and false hopes. With our arrangement, I found a way for you to learn a different life. That was the night I made a pact with our Romany Rye. I suspect this would be a good time to divulge to you his name. His name was Mr. Beaufant. The man until this reading you regarded as your father. Mr. Beaufant was a good man. I had brought many jewels from Romania. (I had never even told your father about them). They had been handed down through my family four generations. Stories told they were from the Royal Family. How they fell into the hands of the Ludar, is another interesting story, but not for you now. I truly was unaware of their value in the Americas, until I had asked Mr. Beaufant to find out their value. He took them on one of his trips to the big Port City (where we had come to on the ship from Romania). He came home and told me they were worth many American dollars. Enough to pay for you to go to an American school, and to pay for our keep with many dollars left over. He said it was worth more than all his land! Can you imagine! So this was our pact. I gave him all the money, to take care of all our expenses. Past, present, and your future. He would buy the same amount of land that he had for you, and build you a house, and each year the tribe could rest there on that land as long as they wanted. He would put half of the remaining money in a bank for you.. (It is like our money pouch, only there is no pouch, there is a building that holds the money until you go to the building and pick it up there). The rest of the money I gave to him because he was such a good man to our people. He said it was too much money. It would pay off his land, and his businesses, and yet he could live without working and not run out. That was okay with me. What he was doing for you was worth any price to me. He promised to raise you as his own daughter. He joked that his wife was having so many babies that most people would never even know she hadn't given birth to you. She had dark hair and dark eyes, just like you! The other part of our pact was that each harvest, when the tribe came, he would let you leave with them for one month so you could learn the life of the travelers. And then he would follow the trail of the tribe a month later and bring you back to your land. I told Mr. Beaufant, I would write this all down for you, and you were to be given this on your fourteenth birthday, when you became a woman. So if you are reading this dear Louisa, you are fourteen, and no doubt very happy to finally learn of your rich inheritance, proud of your true identity, and you will pass all this knowledge on to your own children. You have had the luxury of the outsiders life, and still have been able to travel each year with the Rom. A rich future you have, one of culture and one of finery. Your father Serge', only wanted a good and proud life for you. Thanks to the sacrifices of all your ancestors, and to the kindness of Mr. Beaufant and his family, you have this great heritage to pass on. We love you deeply, Your mother."

Oh but wait. That isn't the end! A very chalky piece of paper falls out of the journal after my sister looks up at me. A letter. It is mildewed and had dirt all over it, but the print is vivid. It is a letter dated October 12, 1908. The return address is at the top of the letter. It is from a Federal Prison. It is a short letter, but it has an explanation we had been looking for. My sister picked it up, (by now almost hoarse) and began reading again.

"To my niece Louisa in the care of Mr. Beaufant,

I am writing you this so there is confirmation for you Louisa, that you know I hold nothing against you for what you are about to be told. Harbor no guilt, because this will waste your life. We in the Ludar, worked too hard to preserve your life, for you to not use it to the full. Mr. Beaufant was in Europe last harvest when we came through to spend our time with you. When the tribe broke camp, and we took you with us as we normally do each year for your visitation, the neighbor man down the road only knew you as Mr. Beaufant's daughter. There was no one there that knew the truth but us. As you know, Mrs. Beaufant died a few years back, and I am afraid the pact between your mother and Mr. Beaufant rested only with Mr. Beaufant and me. The neighbor man obtained a posse to follow us, saying we had stolen you. They came after us and questioned you. You told them you were a Beaufant, because that is all you knew. They arrested me and your other uncle and took us away for kidnapping an American child. The penalty in the laws of the Americas is death. There is nothing you could have done. The secret of the pact was not to be revealed for two more years. Revealing a pact would be worse than death to us. So when you read this it will be in your journal, and we will have met our demise. But this letter is to relieve you of guilt and also to give you our permission to choose the European life if you so choose. The tribe will go through many hard days without a Bora (head of the family) and you have all the advantages of the Beaufant lifestyle. No one will know of this pact after our deaths, but you and Mr. Beaufant himself. He would take the pact to his death if you so ask. It is a choice you have child. You can wrap your cards in the purple cloth and never use them again, and we would understand. We love you greatly, and we pray that you keep the Rom with you, if only in your heart. Uncle Romi"

I sat on the floor of that pantry and looked at my sister. Neither one of us could speak! My sister began to put the cards back in the box, and fold up the letter. She slowly wrapped them back up. First in the red cloth, putting the gold ropes around them, and then in the purple suede cloth, and tied the brown thin leather straps around the package one at a time. I looked at her as if for the first time, Her dark eyes and dark hair. I instantly thought of our mother and things started making sense. Her love for music and dancing, and jewelry. She had a ring on every finger and always wore gold ankle bracelets. The thing that made the most sense was why my grandmother had been so hateful. She made a choice to deny her heritage, to hide what she was. It must have been a very hard fight. Considering she was only fighting herself. No one else knew. The actual trick would have been to enjoy her life! To live the game to the full! But she played the game with the wrong motives. The tricks of the gypsies was based on the cleverness of the mind. To create illusions for the joy and happiness of others. But if your game caused harm or pain, you would lose. The illusion would fade, the trick would be discovered. She deprived her children of the rich heritage her mother and Mr. Beaufant spent so many years to protect. She spent her life trying to protect her lie. Even to the extent of her white face powder she wore till the day she died! My mind was racing, and then my sister broke the silence.

"Do you get it?" she said with a smile on her face.

I said, "Get what?"

She went on, " If she really wanted this to be a secret she would have destroyed all this when she was fourteen. She saved this, and hid this, for us to find! She knew someday someone in her family would discover this!"

I looked at my sister with rings on both hands, and the bright red and orange scarf tied in her dark hair, and just smiled. Grandma had taken Uncle Romi's suggestion is all. The people that meant the most to her were all gone. She had her land, and her money, and the Beaufant name. She had the cleverness of the mind all right. But there was the option she had to destroy the evidence. Why did she leave that one path to her secret? Why would she leave the book that told the truth about what she was hiding? And then it hit me! She hadn't denied anything! She was part of the Rom through and through. What good is a trick if no one knows it's been played? That's why she had to leave the book. So we all knew….she had played the greatest trick of all!

The Horn Player

There is something to be said for those that live their dream –
The player of the Horn,
who went hungry, watched loved ones walk away
Until someone finally listened to his song one day
And now he plays with pride-
Satisfied
that the sacrifices were worth the life he now lives.
Unaware of those of us who listen with admiration,
Those of us who dreamed without the courage-
Those of us who called the loved one back,
and succumbed to their happiness rather than our own.
Realizing with each note he plays-
of each wrong decision we made that left us in the audience-
rather than on the stage.
Play on – Play on
Oh you with your convictions
Share all your struggle with those of us-
Who truly hear your life in your horn.
Play on, as you're no longer dreaming
And they are playing your song.

The Pirate Story

I have to admit when I took on the job of running a Bed and Breakfast on the Beach I didn't think I would find a great deal of suspense and intrigue. I am learning not to assume anything in my not so old age......

Many have asked why the B & B was named the Princess Inn...and I decided to go on the journey to find out! Well you won't believe where it took me!!!! To the attic, upstairs above the third floor...I was looking around up there for some boxes we had stored and found an old dirty leather volume strapped with a leather string...laying up under a two by four...it belonged to a Sea Captain named Mr. Avery Heathrow III. All I could do is sit down and begin reading – and the following is exactly what I read –

His very life was the sea, the journal says. Apparently, he had sailed back and forth between the Americas and Europe buying and selling things, and was very successful at it. He only believed in fun and adventure. There were rumors that he would walk his ship and inquire of the men if they were happy in their works of servitude to him. If they weren't he would throw them overboard! "Better to have a fun swim, then to work at a job unhappily!" Well, it seemed he had an unfortunate encounter with our local pirate Blackbeard, who was known for lying in wait in the InterCoastal Waterways, waiting to see the Tops of Sails (hence the name Top Sail Island) so that he could overtake them... a battle ensued, and Mr. Avery Heathrow escaped by the skin of his teeth.

The journal says his ship was completely lost and he was lying there, injured with pieces of the ship crashing up against him. He writes that through his blurred vision he caught a glimpse of long black hair, so long it was cascading across his broken arm. He felt cold cloths on his face, and remembers someone trying to give him water. Days evidently passed and he woke up to find himself in a well lit room, sun shining in over his blankets, and a warm summer breeze flowing thru the open window. There was a shadow in the door way, a vision once again of the long black hair almost touching the ground. As she approached the bed, he caught the sight of her face. She was undoubtedly the most beautiful woman he had ever seen. Her exotic tan colored skin and her eyes a very curious greenish gray. She handed him an envelope with out a word. It was a message from his sponsors in Europe. They had heard of his misfortune and had issued another ship that would arrive in two weeks to pick him up. When he looked up to ask where he was, she had disappeared ……..again…Funny thing was.. it didn't seem like she had time to even walk out the door….Who was she and …...where was he?????

He continues, " as I lay here, I have decided I must get up, this laying around I am just not good at. As I try to sit up, I begin to realize my arm and leg are injured. I find it difficult to move the way I need to - but I must. My ship is coming in , (Is that where that cliché' came from?) in two weeks! I am curious of this lady that has been weaving in and out of my dreams...Only a short time to get to know her."

He somehow got up from his sick bed, and there was a very convenient cane laying next to the table, as well as sandals and clothes, (his exact size), however clearly not his. He gets up, and puts on the very "un-sea-captain" like clothes. (Or is it un-Pirate " like clothes???) He speaks of them being extremely soft. Unlike anything he had ever had in his lifetime.

He walked on out to the veranda, and found the house sitting on a beautiful spot of land, live oaks twisting close to the sand, with the waves crashing up on the beach in front of him ....and there in his view is the woman...with her dark hair flowing, walking on the beach. He made it over to her, limp and all, introducing himself and she told him only one name, that she is called "Lahela." When she began talking freely, she would catch herself and realize she was revealing too much somehow, and then they sit down on her blanket. She then hands him a pendant he obviously recognized. It was a gift from the Queen and she had found it in the sand. She confessed that she lived alone in the huge house, but it obviously had not always been that way. She offered him some of the wine her father had made years ago. He asked if he can keep the cork for reasons he chooses not to reveal....and then Cap't Avery, being totally captivated by her enchanting eyes....begins to tell her of some of his adventures and how he has planned his revenge on Black Beard. He must get back what was taken from him... He will attack him and his crew and take him for ransom to the Queen, as soon as his "ship comes in…" (there we go again!) She, without a word, wipes a tear from her eye, and gets up slowly and walks away - He writes that he is puzzled once again by his elucid black haired Princess. But he is puzzled by many things.

" I am beginning to yearn for the sea", he writes, "and I wonder how most people stay on land to live out their lives. I think not even my God could tame me to live this life. To eat and sleep and never smell the open sea…"

It seems many days have passed now since his last entry -

He has been fishing, healing, and having afternoon picnics on the Beach with his lady friend Miss Lahela. They have been getting on quite famously and with apparently no indiscretions. She has revealed to him that her father was a Man of the Sea, and had also succumbed to Pirates but had not faired well. Or I guess hadn't faired at all. Thus all the drama and tears and so forth. His ship is expected to come in any day (too easy….) and so they are preparing their goodbyes. He thinks he has been on this island at least a month or longer, and Miss Lahela has treated him as a part of her non existent family since he had been there.

He says he will never forget her hearty breakfasts she served him, and always a curious dish of yogurts and pineapples and other fruits.

He is leaving, and she can not convince him to stay. However he states, "I know it is the manner of Men of the Sea, to make promises to return to fair maidens. But she has captivated some part of my soul. I am going to leave with out the promise, but I will be back. When I find Black Beard, I will run him into the ground in front of his very house, and for all to see. Then I will come back to my Princess on the "Ile de Plaisir" (French—Island of Pleasure or could be "Pleasure Island" , which is the Island we are on right now!). I write this as a vow, this seventeenth day of August, 1717 year of our Lord that I will return to my Princess Lahela" Well, it is apparent that Lahcla was upset and was not comforted at all by Mr. Avery Heathrow III, as he boarded his new ship the following day. He thanked her, and said good by as she stood on the beach waving. He said he must go, and made no promises. She stood on the beach and watched them as they pulled anchor, and they turned the ship north and left her standing there. "You could see the Big house over the trees" he said, "sort of standing as a Beacon for weary travelers. So close to the water sailors could row right up to her porch." He watched in the twilight as the candles were being lit around the house, and out on the Beach. He imagined her every move as she went thru the house, closing this window and leaving that one open. She would soon get a glass of her father's wine, and walk towards the beach and spend this evening alone. But not for long, he writes...Black Beard wasn't far away....only a few miles north, in the Topsail Inlet. He would never know what hit him....

It really wasn't a long sail, by the better of the day, he says, he was already on the outskirts of the inlet where the Pirates were rumored to be making a home– The fine gentlemen laid back waiting until dark before their approach he says—and then they slowly crept towards the overwhelming ship—the sound of the pirate's voices were flowing over the ocean. They are all yelling, laughing, and drinking, and quite unaware that their doom was right behind them. Mr. Avery advances to the rear of the other ship and starts blasting away —some of Avery's men jump aboard the pirate ship and the fight was on—Blackbeard himself confronts Sir Avery, and Avery corners him in the bow of the boat - the goings back and forth seem gruesome to repeat, but the outcome was probably quite a sight. Blackbeard and his men try to escape by water, and run their ship a ground—when they realize they are stuck in the sandbar below—they all begin to jump over into the water. It seems even funny to Avery, as they are jumping into the water like scared rabbits, many of them are getting stuck in the very sand their ship is sitting in. These brave, fearless Pirates, that had frightened so many, stealing what ever they could see, and left people dead, dying or wanting to be dead, are now running for their very lives. Sir Avery says it looked like little girls running from a field mouse. He says, " before letting this scoundrel run with his life, I had to let him know who was sinking his ship. I left orders that no one would take the spoils, it would be impossible to return these riches to their rightful owners, so all the jewels and gold sank with the Queen Anne..(IS HE NUTS????? Me an Avery would have had words about diamonds floating to the floor of the sea.).So, this makes sense. Historical records show us that Blackbeard ran ashore right in front of his own house at Topsail Inlet., just north of Pleasure Island, in North Carolina. The name of his ship was the "The Queen Ann's Revenge". They say he did it on purpose so he could steal all of the treasures for himself. Captain Avery knows better. He writes, "as I watched them all jump from the stern, I had to laugh. It was almost comical. Waiting a few minutes, to see that all had left, I then order the canon's to fire. As they began hitting the "Queen Anne", a curious thing happened. I looked at the railing of the ship and saw a lady standing there. Her black hair blowing, a familiar face, it seemed....she had a sad look, and was doing nothing to save herself. As I ran to get closer I realized it was my precious Princess Lahela. Standing there bound by tethers. But how? I had left her on the Beach miles away. Blackbeard and I had not crossed paths, he was sitting here on our arrival..... A Loud noise ensued, the ship fell in pieces, and she was gone."

Now, according to the Journal - he has basically hijacked his own ship and they are sailing back to the cove where he had originally left Lahela on the beach, 60 miles south of Topsail. He's going to see if Blackbeard left anything of her house. Anything. He must have captured her somehow – although none of it makes sense.... As they pull into the cove—he saw smoke billowing thru the trees. So, now let's see what he has written.

"As I ordered the anchor to be dropped I could feel the tension in my men. They resented this detour, and were trying very hard to obey, although they felt this all frivolous, knowing that Blackbeard leaves nothing in his path of destruction. I jumped down to the small boat so I could get to land and then began running as soon as my feet hit the sand. I ran thru the dunes, and got to the clearing, and lo and behold, there stands the great house, unscathed. I stood in shock, not sure of what I was seeing. I walk to the back of the house and see a fire burning—but it is a smoldering fire in the ground—one that is used for cooking. I also see a figure bent over the fire, in bright colored clothing. As I get closer I see the figure stand up, and as it turns I see this long black hair fall over her shoulder, and as she turns slowly I see it is her. My Princess Lahela is standing before me. I can't believe my eyes! I run to her and she is real, it isn't a vision this time. I tell her I thought her dead that I had seen her likeness on the ship, "The Queen Anne", before it sank, and in all my babbling, she laughs. She calls me close to crazy, and laughs. She said that it was an excuse to come back to her....that I had found a love stronger than my love for the sea. So here I am today, with my Princess. I let my ship sail on, I realized I had been caught in the fiercest net there is for a sailor. Love. The kind that no matter what port you sail in to—you will see her there—so where could a ship take you? I had found the most beautiful place and the most beautiful woman—the search for my adventures had ended on this island.—I will live out my days with My Princess on this little Pleasure island." And there you have it.

As I sat and thought about what I read that day – I found many things curious, as I am sure you did yourself. Was Lahela real? Why did she keep fading in and out of places, and showing up on the sinking ship? Just how long had she been at this house? Why don't they mention Sir Avery in the history of the demise of Blackbeard, and why haven't they ever found the jewels from the Queen Anne? Was Avery a pirate or a worthy sea captain? What was he saving those corks for?

Well, some things are just left for us to wonder about I guess ….unless there is another journal somewhere – hhhmmmmm - I'll keep looking and let you know…..

If Only In A Dream

If only in a dream I could see you
If only in a dream I could see your face
As the hours turn I wish I could take the space besides you
And that would be okay, and I could get through another day

If only in a dream I could feel you
If only in a dream your laughter is all I hear
I'm longing for the time I feel your arms around me
Now that would be okay, if that's the only way

As for now – my loneliness surrounds me
What I feel – is tearing out my heart
As for now – I'll toss and turn and wonder
If just the nearness of you could satisfy me

If only in a dream I could hear you
If only in a dream you'd say you love me
I'd search to find a secret place where we could be together
And that would be okay – if that could just be today

As for now – a dream is all I know
I close my eyes, hoping you'll be there
I believe my prayers will bring the answer
I'm wishing on a star and hoping in my heart

If only in a dream I could touch you
If only in a dream I could see your face
If that's the only way….
    I'll just dream my life away……...

Teach Them To Fish……

Believe it or not, I've had my moments when I sit and wonder why my life has been so hard. What choices did other people make, that took them in a such a different, (and much easier) direction. But reality is I have three small children, divorced, and working 473 jobs, to pay the rent, feed my children, and then I decide each month if I want to pay the light bill or car payment. Reality in fact comes very quickly every single morning. I work as a student nurse in ICU, gagging at just about everything I have to do, wondering if I will ever be able to go back to school. I take care of dying people everyday, hopefully not being the cause of their demise. I go home and fix dinner, help with homework, do baths, read stories, and lights out at 8:30pm. I put clothes out for school, I make lunches, and at 9:30pm, make one loop through the bedrooms to check on the kids, yes, they are all asleep. The door bell rings, it is the babysitter, and I am off, to the second job. I do the accounting at the local Jewelry store at the Mall. I gaze constantly at the beautiful rings and necklaces, all of which I will never own. And if I had the money would I really buy it anyway? One of those rings would pay my rent for 5 or 6 months. People are walking around with my rent on their fingers. It just doesn't make sense.

So, I get done with their books by midnight, leave by 12:30am, and get home by 1am.. I go in each room, and feel their backs, yes all three are breathing, and then I watch T.V. until I fall asleep, so I can wake the kids up at 6am, and start all over. This goes on and on everyday, not just for me but for all the single Mom's I work with. We all move to the big city to make a living, and we do make more money! But we pay more to live here. You pay any extra money you may have in babysitters, because now you are not around any family who use to babysit for free….what a tangled web we weave when we don't think before conceive…..So life goes on… I always have plans on how we are going to all break out of this invisible prison we have been convicted to, and despite the "great dead beat dad" program for child support, none of us seem to receive any.…

I always dreamed about winning some big amount of money and what I would do with it…in fact that was usually how I would fall asleep at night. Who I would give it to , who I wouldn't….but then there again lies the futility, I couldn't win candy at a cake walk…..nothing, ever, never…..never won a thing….because that is my life you see….or it was anyway.

For years, my busy life had been fueled by diet soda. That is how I woke up, and ran thru my day… caffeinated. How bizarre then that all those quarters in a soda machine would tie in so neatly to my future. It was a usual morning, and a usual chaotic day. I had dropped all appropriate children at appropriate schools (at least I hope I did) and was on my way to work. I made the usual stop for my diet soda…..and was trying to enjoy my ride in traffic…at least 45 minutes to an hour each morning. I cherished this time I spent in traffic, alone with the goofy guys on the radio. I would finish my make up at all the traffic gridlocks, and could calculate the traffic on the freeway by how many nails I got painted waiting on the on ramp for the freeway to clear for incoming traffic.. I was multi-talented.

As I listened to the radio, the DJ starts talking about the big YA YA Diet Soda contest, and how he was going to be the one to win the fifty million dollars! I was listening, sort of....until he said to pull off the rapper and look on the back of the paper. It sounded like he was talking directly to me. I took the plastic bottle, I pull off the paper, and you guessed it – It is saying that I am the Grand Prize Winner. It is saying that I have won 50 million dollars! I, like you at this point, was saying "okay, what's the joke…" Of course, multi-talented as I am, I almost wreck my car. I had to pull off the Freeway. As soon as I did that of course, the little CHIP car (California Highway Patrol) pulls over right behind me....I am screaming and he is trying to see what is wrong with me.,....he calls for back up, because someone is having a nervous break down on the 101 freeway. "WHO???", I am trying to ask. I continue to scream, and then cry, and then scream some more...Meanwhile cop cars are collecting behind me… and now they are calling an ambulance…they have put big orange cones all around my car and even in the slow lane. At this point I open the car door to try to get out and quite comically they all fall to the ground with their guns out…I am not sure why that looked so funny to me, but all I could do was laugh. I try to tell them I am okay, but they don't believe me...They are screaming at me to get back in the car. That was even funnier.... Now, I am hearing helicopters over head. The goofy guys on the radio are saying there is a traffic jam on the 101. They say there is some lady in a car having a nervous breakdown it seems...in a silver cellica....The next thing I know there are paramedics trying to get me out of the car...They have put oxygen on my face, and I am pulling it off, they put it back on, I pull it back off. .I finally thru my laughter, get out a whisper that I just won fifty million dollars. The guy says, "Sure you did ma'am." I said, 'no, I am serious! I just won the YA YA Diet Soda Contest. I have the rapper right here!" I show it to him, and he begins to get more excited then me! He laughs and yells to the other guys that I really am okay...he starts to tell them what all the commotion is about...and I am overcome with some sort of sensibility. It hits me, that I don't want anyone to know. I mean no-one. It isn't really thought out, but I know that I could do much more with the money silently than publicly. Come on now, I have been dreaming about this one for along time. I have the whole plan down, a million different ways. I just never thought I would get the chance to deploy it.

I turn to the policeman and said, "What is one thing you have always wanted and you knew you could never afford …" "My own Harley"…he said with a grin. I said "Well, if you will write down your name and address, I will see that you get one, if you promise to keep my identity a secret." He said, No, ma'am I can't accept…"

"Yes you can"...I said with a loud urgency, "a Harley, free and clear? Yes you can...write down your info, quick. and cover me on this....please" Right then, his partner walks towards the car, "Jeff, what's going on, does she need a transport?" No man, she was just excited about...... um.....her boyfriend...ahh...asked her to marry him... she was overwhelmed....but she is okay now, aren't you ma'am?" "Yes sir, I am sorry for all the confusion, I just got a little excited is all". "Are you okay to drive, Ma'am", Jeff asks. "Oh yes, I think I can pull it together now,", and he slips a business card into my hand. "Well, okay then, let us get you back on the road...I will keep the orange cones up until you get back in traffic...You take care now, and congratulations" "Thank you, officer.." I wipe my eyes, and pick up my cell as I start to drive back on the road. I call the number on the back of the label, and speak to an Agent that takes the serial number on the paper, and then checks his computer and tells me to report immediately to an office in downtown LA. I tell them I will be there shortly, and only make one other phone call. To my job. No, I didn't quit, I just called in sick....and said I would see them tomorrow. So, this is where my journey began. This is where my path for life opened up to me. This is where I remembered the story about the fish.. If you give a man a fish, he eats for the day. If you teach a man to fish, he will eat for a lifetime.

I went to the Contest office, and spent the next 4 and ½ hours there. I swear, I never had to prove who I am in so many different ways, so many times in my life.

Yes, these ears are mine. I was born to my mother. I am who my birth certificate , social security, drivers license, light bill, phone bill, hospital ID say I am....yes, these shoes belong to me.. Good grief! After all that, they call my bank to arrange the transfer of funds, and to warn them that my measley little bank account (that was on the verge of being closed because it had been over drawn for a month) is about to have a rather large deposit. After they take fees, and all the taxes out I still end up with $34,995,000.00. Are you kidding me? Why does the government get fifteen million dollars??? Because they have done so much for me as a single mom? I have to catch myself – like I have had thirty four million dollars before ! I need to shut up! I still am not believing any of this. I could have made a lot more if I had agreed to let them use "my likeness" in their advertising, but that would ruin my plan for my "Teach Them To Fish" game. I did agree to the radio advertising, because they promised to keep my full name off the air. Cool. So some girl, named Sarah, was now a millionaire. Now, that all the paperwork was done, I am now walking out of their office, thinking to myself, okay...what do I do now? Oh, I am suppose to go directly to the bank, because they have to talk to me regarding investments, and all this other stuff. All I keep thinking is – I want some lobster and champagne. I am thinking I would love to have Lobster Thermadour from Allieo's on the Wharf in San Francisco. My next thought is, sure that would be nice but who can afford that? Then, I think again…"OH YEAH ….I CAN!!!!!!!!

I go on to the Bank. Everyone has great idea's of what I should do and what I could do, and I get the instructions of how I can spend it and how I can't. I had them set up a credit card, give me a check book, a little cash, and I ran out of the place, This is not the day for wise investments. It has to be a day of much fun! This day would be for me and mine. The Game would start tomorrow.

My personal indulgences that day were minimal. I asked the kids what they wanted to do. They were hungry, (Pinks for Hot Dogs) and wanted to go to the movies. As I watched them eat their hot dogs, I decided at that moment, they would not know either. We would gradually improve our lifestyle, but nothing too noticeable. I didn't want them to change as people. I loved the way they were. I truly believed that their compassion for people, and love between them was because we had always struggled. I didn't have the right to throw something in the game that most grown ups can't handle. "Teach them to Fish" had to be just my game, not theirs, at least not now. Note to self….buy Harley tomorrow and have delivered to Officer Jeff…

Next day came bright and early, especially since I had slept all of about two hours. How could I sleep? The dream I used to go to sleep with most of my life had come true! So now what? I would have to come up with something else. My something else that night was, "What about this? And What about that?.."

I rushed the kids thru breakfast and we started off for our usual routine. I had decided my "illness" was going to last just one more day. The kids piled into the car and were ready for their normal school day - and then I turned to the on ramp of the freeway. My two oldest say – "Hey Mommy, where are you going, this isn't the way to school!" I said, " I know, I have to run an errand first so you'all have to go with me. Do you really care if you are a little late for school?" They all laughed, and were game for being late. Well, Disneyland was only a half hour away….some place that Mr. Disney built for kids, and then after he died, his corporation made it too expensive for most of them to go. I could never afford to take mine there They weren't paying much attention, until we drove into the big parking lot and they saw the sign – they were afraid to assume that they were coming there to play. So my son very coyly said, "Mommy is this the errand you have to run?" and I laughed and told them to put their books away because today we were all playing hooky! I couldn't get them to stop screaming, my youngest daughter would scream for awhile and then say " what's hooky?" and then scream some more…..Well, needless to say we stayed until the kids almost had to carry me back to the car – we had so much fun…..we swore on a bag of potato chips that this would be our little family secret and that tomorrow would be a normal day! And it was. Everybody up and in the car and I heard little giggles all the way to their schools….I made my everyday stop to get my diet coke.(Man! I would drink this for ever now!) And then I worked my way thru traffic to get to my job. Flashing back on the hilarity of the day before, when I first found out I had won, and all those guys dropping to the ground when I tried to get out of my car! I would order Officer Jeff's Harley from work....and just see how the day proceeds. I didn't truly know what else to do. If I thought about it too much, I would get very nervous. The concept of all that money was mind bending. Nothing had sunk in.

As I am getting coffee in the Employee Lounge a girl I worked with, Gretchen, was wiping her eyes and looking out a window. I walked over to her, and asked her what was wrong. She told me that she was late to work again, and they told her if she was late one more time she would get fired. I asked her, why she was late, and she proceeded to tell me that the car she had just bought three months ago, from an easy credit lot , had just fallen on the ground on the freeway. The axel had broken, and she couldn't get it fixed. She didn't know how she was going to get to work tomorrow either. I know this is where you think I run to the rescue and buy her a new car. But I had learned in millionaire school the day before, the government comes down on you when you start just giving money away. Besides that wasn't really going to help her. We needed to talk. So, I offered to pick her up the next day, and give her rides to and from work until she figured some things out. This way, we would have time to talk, and I could see what was at the bottom of her crisis. As the days progressed, Gretchen and I really got into some nitty gritty conversations. It seemed she had never finished high school , got married too young, and basically had children before she had a future. She had always wanted to be a photographer. A professional one for a newspaper or magazine . But instead she was working at this office job, barely getting by. It all sounded too familiar. I went home that night and had to figure out my game plan, she would be my first project.

A few weeks had passed when Gretchen actually came into my cubicle at work so excited! She had won a contest at a restaurant we had gone to for lunch a few weeks back. The prize was a very expensive camera. How ironic she was saying that she had won a camera. I told her about a contest I had read about that she could enter pictures in. The contest winner could win a full scholarship to UCLA's Photography School. She was ready for all of it. I told her to come by my office the next morning and I would give her the numbers and contact people. I hadn't seen her smile this much in all the time we had worked together.

As we pulled up in front of her house that evening, a neighbor who was an older man walked slowly up to the car. He said he knew she had no car now, and that a remarkable thing had happened. His brother had developed an eye problem, and could no longer drive, so he gave him his SUV. It was only two years old, and he was wondering if she would be interested in the car. She said she was interested, but she had no money. He said, neither do I, and he tossed her the keys. He said he couldn't drive two cars, and his mama had taught him to share, and he walked away. We both got out of my car and ran across the street, to look at the SUV. She couldn't believe what was happening! She opened the car and looked in the glove box. There was a plastic envelope inside, that usually holds the registration. She opened it to see who the man was, and pulled out the registration. She got a look of almost terror on her face, and handed me the paper. The car was in her name. I asked her where this man lived? She said she wasn't sure. I haven't really seen him around. I thought he came from the house across the street, that the car was parked in front of. Gretchen walked up to the door, and an older lady answered the door. Gretchen asked if her husband was home, and she said she didn't have a husband, and no one lived there with her. She then asked Gretchen if that was her car outside. Gretchen said, she believed it was, and the old woman asked her to move her car, and shut the door. She then looked at me and asked me what I thought she should do, and I told her to drive the car into her driveway. She could go to DMV the next day, and make sure the car was legally hers. If it was, be happy, and call it a day.

    MAN! My game was really getting to be fun! Of course you know by now the setups. Or maybe you need to go back and find them – but nothing was by chance. But the great thing is - she didn't know, and will never know, and this little boost was all she needed. She was taking it all and running with it. It was obvious no one had given her a hand up before. She now had a future – not because of me, but because of the choices she was now making. It was like she had made it through a maze and was now on the other side. I got an e/mail that afternoon. It was an invitation to a going away party at the restaurant down the street. It was something the company always did when someone was leaving in good graces. The owners would take everyone out to lunch their last day. The exciting thing was the party was for Gretchen. She had won the grant for her Photography education at UCLA. A full scholarship. Amazing, don't you think?

Well, the next few weeks proved a little dull, except for a thank you card from Officer Jeff for his new Harley. I kept working and inserting new things very casually into our life that would go unnoticed. I mean small things. I bought a new t.v. to replace the two that were sitting on top of each other in the living room. (one for the picture, one for the sound). I looked for a modest house in a better neighborhood and finally found one that would work for all of us. The kids didn't realize of course that I had bought it, and I didn't mention that to anyone at work either. They were gradually getting new clothes to replace their hand-me-downs, and I actually bought a full set of new dishes. And real drinking glasses. (the plastic red cups I held onto however....)

Then after a few weeks of just basking in the excitement of the Gretchen project, it was amazing to me, how it seemed the world around me had transformed in to a big playground for my game. Everywhere I went, turned into a challenge of how I could help someone's situation without getting detected.

Simple things, like an afternoon at the bank. I was sitting on the couch in the waiting area, waiting to meet with my advisor, and overheard this conversation between this bank teller and who I assume was her supervisor. I was looking at a magazine, and I guess they thought I wasn't paying any attention. I hear the teller's voice crack, and I look up to see her eyes watering, and she is telling him that she had made a simple mistake, and she had worked there five years and this had never happened before. She had apparently misplaced a check for $265.00. She was now crying and saying she couldn't afford to lose her job over it , and she didn't have the money. She had looked everywhere for it This really hit home to me, because I had done accounting for years, and there had been many times, that the bank in their processing misplaces checks and came up with them weeks later. It's hard telling where the check could have gone. (In the trash was a possibility.) I felt so bad for this girl. She is sitting in this office, with the door open baring her soul to this creep, about how she is a single mom, and she has a family to support – and he sits there smugly with her future in his hands – or so he thinks.

Well, this would be difficult. I sat until he seemed finished with her, and she walked out and went back to her station around the corner. I got up and walked over to her and said I needed to cash a check. She was trying to act like she hadn't been crying, and I just said, I didn't know this bank treated their employees this way. She said that you would get fired if your drawer was short only one time, and she began to whimper and say I can't lose my job, I have a little boy, and they won't tell me if I am getting fired or not, they say they will let me know. I need to know now. I need to know if they are going to fire me. Out of the blue I said to her, "If you had some money would you put your money in stocks or CD's?" She immediately started telling me the pro's and cons of each and how you can make the most interest – I mean this girl was brilliant! I asked her what her name was – it was Jody. I thanked her for her advise, and left the bank. I went back to work realizing I had not accomplished anything at the bank that I had gone for. Jody's situation had troubled me so....

Three days passed before I could get back around to going back to the bank to sit down with the advisor. I went back to plop down on the couch and noticed my advisor (the one who had gone off on Jody three days ago), was no longer in his office. They were putting a new name tag on the door, and Jody was carrying boxes in and out of the room. When I walked up to her, she was smiling and said she would be with me in a minute. I ask her what was going on and she pulled me to the side and said, "You wouldn't believe it! Apparently, the other day, some wealthy person came into the bank and complained about the way Mr. Jones was talking to me.

They threatened to pull thirty million dollars out of the bank because they felt he was rude to me! They even told the Bank President that they wanted me to handle their accounts personally! He fired Mr. Jones on the spot and basically gave me his job! Between me and you, I have been doing most of his job for him for the last three years. He was always asking me for advise. So, when I heard that they were upset with him, I went in and told the Bank President the truth. I stood up for myself for the first time in my life! I had been doing all of his financials and P & L's and they listened to me! Isn't that something!"

"What did they decide to do about the missing money?" "Well, she said," interestingly enough, the money showed up just like you said it would. They came up to me the next day and said the money had shown up in the second count of the drawer. I don't know how, but I'm not one to look a gift horse in the mouth! So, what can I do for you today?" I couldn't reveal myself to her, so I would have to find another financial advisor at the bank and be more discreet about my dealings now. But that was okay with me. I said, "well nothing, Miss Supervisor, I will just go on over here to the teller, and cash my check…you are out of my league now girl!" She laughed and it was a great, deep laugh. You could see the joy and relief on her face. I might have evened the playing field but she ran for the goal on her own.

Well, that was ten years ago, and I am still playing my game with much success. I have had a few close calls but I haven't been discovered yet. Instead of looking for opportunities I just wait for them to find me, and trust me they do! I did finally give up the job. That was really noble and all, but that getting up every morning when I knew I didn't have to – it got to me after awhile. I just invested in some foreclosed houses and started fixing them up. Before long I owned enough to justify my secure lifestyle. My children still don't know either, although they do appreciate the fact that they are eating more than macaroni and cheese and hot dogs these days. And the part of the game that is the most fun? Is that you don't know me either. When things come together for you, will you wonder now if you have met me? Crossed my path somehow? Did I hear you talking in a restaurant to a friend, or over a coffee machine in some office…. When good things happen to you…and you feel you have finally made it…..will you wonder if someone was teaching you to fish??? Well, regardless of how you get there, when you do, always remember to carry an extra fishing pole …..

Freedom Cage

The freeness of one's heart
                In the confines of the earth
The freeness of one's body
                In the confines of their birth
The wanting of perfection
                And the yearning to express
The love one has for many
                Kept in the confines of their death.

J LEE BROWN grew up in a small southern town, and moved to LA where she lived for over 20 years. She has been writing since she was a child, and has recently written a script called Blue Eyes Blind, that is taken from her first novel "Colorblind" which is based on her life. She is directing and producing the film (Blue Eyes Blind) independently next year. She writes from her own personal experiences and likes to call it fiction, and when you read her fictional stories you hopefully find optimism, love and courage in her characters. She is a mother of three, and was a single mother for many of those years, and a grandmother of nine and loving every minute of it.. Although, being a baby boomer, there is nothing conventional about this grandma! She is now living on the Atlantic Coast running a Bed and Breakfast in her spare time! Look for more of her work in the near future.

Printed in the United States
69408LVS00001B/49-54